An Easy-Read Activity Book

American Indian Games and Crafts

by Charles L. Blood

illustrated by Lisa Campbell Ernst

Franklin Watts
New York/London/Toronto/Sydney
1981

R.L. 2.6 Spache Revised Formula

The publisher wishes to acknowledge
the invaluable assistance of Mary Jane Lenz,
Curatorial Assistant, The Museum of the American Indian,
in the preparation of this book.

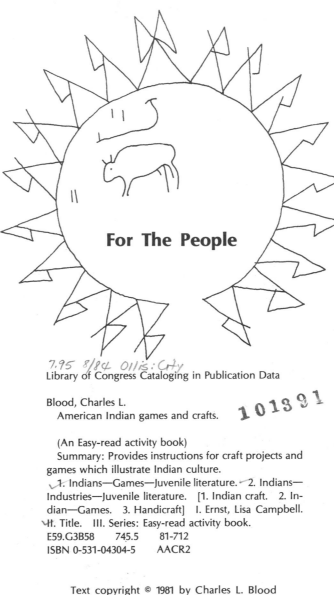

For The People

Library of Congress Cataloging in Publication Data

Blood, Charles L.
  American Indian games and crafts.

  (An Easy-read activity book)
  Summary: Provides instructions for craft projects and
games which illustrate Indian culture.
  1. Indians—Games—Juvenile literature. 2. Indians—
Industries—Juvenile literature. [1. Indian craft. 2. In-
dian—Games. 3. Handicraft] I. Ernst, Lisa Campbell.
II. Title. III. Series: Easy-read activity book.
E59.G3B58   745.5   81-712
ISBN 0-531-04304-5   AACR2

Contents

Before Columbus landed in the Americas in 1492,
the people he called "Indians"
called themselves The People.
After all this time, some still do.

The People had symbols for many things in 1492.
Some painted them on animal skins.
Some carved them in wood.
Some scratched them in stone.

Making Signs and Symbols

You will need:
plain white paper or cloth
crayons, paint, or ink

Paint the designs any way
   you choose.

Playing a Stick Game

You will need:
3 flat sticks (like popsicle
   sticks)
crayons

Make two sticks red on one
   side like this:

 snake

Leave the other side plain.
Make one stick blue on one
   side like this:

man

Leave the other side plain.

How to Play and Score:
Hold all three sticks in both hands.
Toss them in the air.
If all the plain sides fall face
   up, score 4 points.
If all the marked sides land face
   up, score 4 points.
Two Snakes and one plain
   up, score 6 points.
Two plain and one Snake
   up, score 6 points.
One plain, one Snake, and
   one Man up, score 0 points.

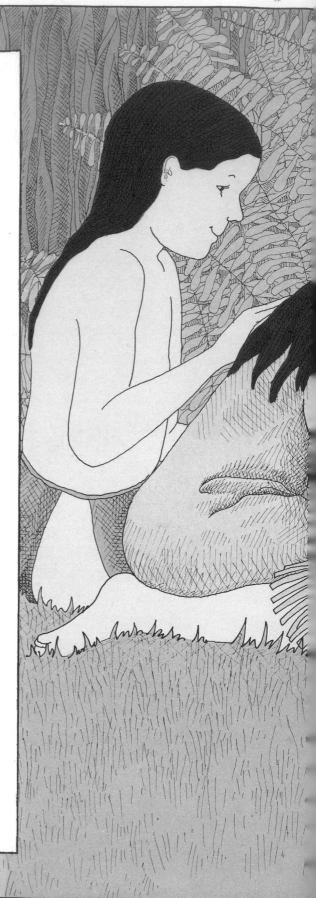

The People liked to play games for fun in 1492.
Some played with stones.
Some played with sticks.
Some played with fruit pits.
Some played with bits of animal bones.

The People lived in many kinds of homes in 1492.
Some were made of clay.
Some were made of logs and mud.
Some were made of animal hides.
Sometimes they decorated the walls.

Making a Wall Hanging

You will need:
different shades of
   construction paper
scissors
glue or paste
1 large piece of
   cardboard or plain
   cloth

Cut one piece of paper into sixteen pieces the same
   shape and size.

Cut another piece of paper into sixteen pieces the
   same shape and size.

Cut a third piece of paper into strips ½″ (1.32 cm) wide.

Cut a fourth piece of paper into strips ½″ (1.32 cm)
   wide.

Cut a fifth piece of paper into pieces this shape:

Glue or paste the pieces on the cardboard or cloth.
   Make your own design if you want to. Let it dry and
   then hang it on the wall.

The People liked to play guessing games in 1492.
Some guessed where a ball was hidden.
Some guessed where a stick was hidden.
Some guessed at where almost anything was hidden.

Playing the Hand Game

You will need:
2 small stones
red paint or marker

Paint or mark a red dot on one of the small stones.
Let it dry.

How to Play:
Sit in a circle on a blanket with some friends.
Hold the stones in one hand.
Pass one of the stones to the person at your right.
   Don't let anyone see which stone you pass.
The person to your left has to guess which stone you
   passed. If this person guesses the correct stone,
      give him both stones. Then he has to
         pass the stones on to another person.
            Next, ask someone else to guess. You
            can play as long as you like, but
            the person who guesses the
            correct stone the most number of
            times wins.

Sand Painting Without Sand

You will need:
1 piece of tan sandpaper 12" x 12"
   (30.5 cm x 30.5 cm)
soft pencil
salt, pepper, and paprika
can of clear spray varnish

Draw the design lightly on the
   sandpaper with the soft pencil.
   Keep the sandpaper on a very
   flat surface. Fill in the design
   with salt, pepper, and paprika.
   Make a small cone so you can
   sprinkle the salt, pepper, and
   paprika easily.
Put the background in first, then
   the figure. Use the cone to
   make an outline for your figure.
Hold the spray can about 10"
   (25 cm) above the finished
   painting. Ask an adult to help
   you. Spray and let it dry. Spray
   again, let dry, and spray again.
   Be sure no salt, pepper, or
   paprika can come loose.

Corn Harvest Figure

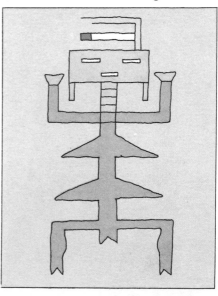

Messenger to the Gods

The People had Medicine Men in 1492.
Some Medicine Men would chant and some would dance.
Some would do both for days and days.
Some would make paintings with different shades of sand.

Playing Arrow Toss

You will need:
50 plastic straws
clay
red paint or permanent marker

clay

Make "arrows" from the straws, by
pushing clay into one end. Paint or mark
the end with the clay inside red.

How to Play:
You need five people. Each person should
have ten arrows. On the ground, draw a
circle that is 3 feet (1 m) across.
Stand two paces from the circle.
The first player should toss his first arrow
into the circle.
The second player tries to toss his arrow
so that it lands on the first player's
arrow. If it does, he wins both arrows. If
it doesn't, the next player tries to land
his arrow on one of the arrows in the
circle. If he does, he wins the arrows
and the game begins again with that
player tossing in the first arrow.
The game continues until someone wins
all the arrows. Or until it gets too dark
to toss any more arrows.

The People liked to play games of skill in 1492.
Some played with hoops.
Some played with knives.
Some played with arrows.

The People believed in a magic bird in 1492.
Some said he had a chest of iron.
Some said lightning came from his eyes.
Some said he made thunder when he flew.

Making a Thunderbird

You will need:
1 piece of heavy cardboard, 16" (40 cm) square
tape
pencil
long pins
papier mâché
paints
(To make papier mâché: Use 1½ cups (0.36 l) of
    wallpaper paste mixed with 2 cups (0.48 l) of water.
    Or ask an adult to boil 1 cup (0.24 l) of white flour
    with 2 cups (0.48 l) of water.)
Draw the thunderbird outline on the cardboard. Stick
    pins in the cardboard. You can put in as many pins
    as you like, as long as they are stuck *inside* the
    outline shape.
Fill in the outline with the wet papier mâché mix.
Let it dry and then paint it. Remove it from the
    cardboard.

The People liked to play dice games in 1492.
Some used dice made of stone.
Some used dice made of wood.
Some used dice made of hard clay.
Some used dice made of bone.

Playing a Wooden Dice Game

You will need:
1 12" (31.68 cm) wooden dowel
small saw
sandpaper
red paint

Ask a grown-up to cut the dowel into three equal
   parts with the saw.
Sand one side of each piece flat.
Paint one round side of one piece to look like this:
These will be the dice.

How to Play:
Throw the dice on a flat surface.
Three round sides up count 10.
Three flat sides up count 5.
Marked stick round side up counts 15.
Plain stick flat side up counts 15.
Everything else counts 0.

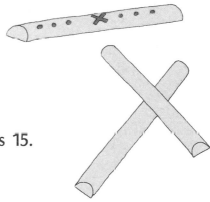

The People danced for many reasons in 1492.
Some danced to the sun.
Some danced to the rain.
Some danced to a good harvest.
Some danced to make people who were sick get well.
Some danced just for fun.

Making a Dancing Bustle

You will need:

construction paper
scissors, string
soft pencil

paint
paste or glue
a round piece of heavy cardboard
14" (30.48 cm) across the middle

Cut twenty pieces of one shade of construction paper to look like a feather 18" (47.52 cm) long.

Cut twenty more pieces of another shade of paper to look like a feather 15" (39.6 cm) long.

With a soft pencil, draw details on the feather. Paint the ends white.

Paste the first twenty feathers around the outside of the cardboard.

Paste the next twenty feathers in a circle around the first circle of feathers.

Cut one circle of red paper 10" (25.40 cm) across the middle.

Cut a circle of black paper 8" (20.32 cm) across the middle.

Cut a circle of white paper 4" (10.16 cm) across the middle.

Paste the white circle on the black circle. Then paste the black circle on the red circle.

Cover the middle of the feathers with the red, black, and white circle.

Punch two holes in the finished bustle. Then run string between the two holes. Make the string long enough so you can tie the bustle around your waist.

The People all made their clothes in 1492.
Some made their clothes with cloth they wove.
Some made their clothes with animal skins.
Everyone made aprons and wore them.

Making an Apron

You will need:
2 iron-on patches
heavy string
scissors
1 piece of white cloth 14" x 14"
    (30.48 x 30.48 cm)
2 strips of iron-on tape 14"
    (30.48 cm) long x 3" (7.6 cm) wide

Cut the patches into strips to make the design.
Ask a grown-up to iron them onto the cloth. Or
    glue them on yourself.
Lay the string across the top of the cloth. Ask a
    grown-up to iron one strip of tape over it. Or you
    can glue it on yourself.
Place the other strip of tape at the bottom of the
    cloth so it overlaps.
Ask an adult to iron on the bottom strip or glue it
    yourself.
Cut the overlap so that it looks like a fringe.
Tie the apron around your waist.

Playing "Shinny"

You will need:

a slim, flexible stick for each player   masking tape
4 sheets of newspaper   red paint
4 strong sticks 15" (38.10 cm) long   string

Bend each slim stick like this:
If you cannot find a stick that bends,
  tape two sticks together.

3 feet

Tie the stick so it will stay bent.
Roll the newspaper into a ball. Cover it with tape.
Paint the design on in red.

How to Play:

Shinny is like hockey, except that there is no net.
Make a goal by putting two of the strong sticks into the
  ground 3 feet (1 m) apart at each end of the playing
  field. (The field should be pretty big, because there is a lot
  of running around in this game.)
To begin, set the ball in the middle of the field. Each team
  stands by the goal. On signal, both teams run to the ball.
The idea is to get the ball through the other team's goal
  markers.
Do not touch the ball with your hands or feet, only with
  the sticks.
You can throw the ball with your shinny stick. But you
  cannot hit the other player with your stick.
One point is scored for each goal. As many can play as want
  to, but there must be the same number on each side.

The People liked to play ball games in 1492.
Some played for a week.
Some played for a day.
Some played for only an hour or two.

The People liked to make bracelets in 1492.
Some made belts.
Some made necklaces.
Some made all of these things.

Making a Necklace

You will need:
macaroni that looks like this:
2 or 3 kinds of food dye
string

Put some of the macaroni into each of the dyes until
  it is the shade you want it. Don't leave the
  macaroni in the dye too long or it will get soggy.
Spread the macaroni out to dry.
Thread it on the string any way you like.

The People wore things to show how brave they were.
They wore beautiful things to show they were rich.
They wore some things for religious reasons.

Some wore signs of bravery on their chests.
Some wore the skin of a Bear or a Buffalo.
Some wore Eagle Feathers.

Making a Breastplate

You will need:
black cardboard (or cardboard painted black)
white plastic straws
red plastic straws
some of the macaroni left over from the necklace
string
scissors

Cut the black cardboard into four pieces 6"
   (15.24 cm) long and 1" (2.64 cm) wide. Punch a
   hole every ¼" (.66 cm) from top to bottom.
Cut the red and white straws into 2" (5 cm) long
   pieces. Make enough to finish the breastplate.
Start at the bottom. Tie a big knot in the string at
   one end.
Run the strips through the bottom hole in one piece
   of cardboard. Add a piece of macaroni. Then add
   a white straw and another piece of macaroni.

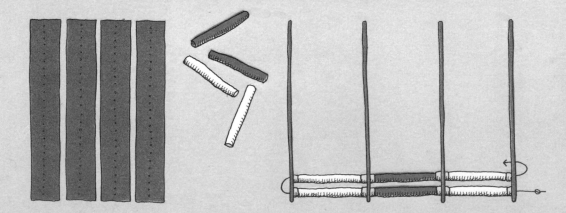

Run the string through the bottom hole in the next
   piece of cardboard. Add a piece of macaroni, a
   red straw, and another piece of macaroni.

Run the string through the third piece of cardboard.
   Add a piece of macaroni, a white straw, and
   another piece of macaroni.

Then run the string through the lowest hole of the
   last piece of cardboard and back through the next
   highest hole. Add pieces of macaroni and straw as
   you work your way up to the top.

When you are done stringing, tie the string in a knot
   at the top of the breastplate. Tie on two more
   pieces of string so you can wear the finished
   breastplate around your neck.

The People lived in many places in 1492.
Some lived in the forest.
Some lived in the mountains.
Some lived by the sea.
Some lived in the desert.
And after all this time...some still do.